Benjamin Breckinridge Warfield

The Gospel of the Incarnation

Two sermons preached in the Chapel of Princeton Theological Seminary,

October 9, 1892, and January 8, 1893

Benjamin Breckinridge Warfield

The Gospel of the Incarnation
Two sermons preached in the Chapel of Princeton Theological Seminary, October 9, 1892, and January 8, 1893

ISBN/EAN: 9783337087777

Printed in Europe, USA, Canada, Australia, Japan

Cover: Foto ©Lupo / pixelio.de

More available books at **www.hansebooks.com**

Princeton Theological Seminary.

THE GOSPEL OF THE INCARNATION.

TWO SERMONS

PREACHED IN THE CHAPEL OF PRINCETON
THEOLOGICAL SEMINARY

October 9, 1892, and January 8, 1893,

BY

BENJAMIN B. WARFIELD,

PROFESSOR IN THE SEMINARY.

NEW YORK:

ANSON D. F. RANDOLPH & COMPANY,

(INCORPORATED)

182 FIFTH AVENUE.

1893.

PRESS OF
EDWARD O. JENKINS' SON,
NEW YORK.

TO THE

STUDENTS OF PRINCETON SEMINARY,

FOR WHOM THEY WERE PREPARED,

TO WHOM THEY WERE PREACHED,

AND ON WHOSE REQUEST THEY ARE NOW PRINTED,

These Sermons

IN THEIR PRINTED FORM

ARE AFFECTIONATELY DEDICATED.

I.

THE END OF THE INCARNATION.

I.

THE END OF THE INCARNATION.

JOHN vii. 38-39: *For I am come down from heaven, not to do mine own will, but the will of Him that sent me; and this is the will of Him that sent me, that of all that He hath given me, I should lose nothing, but should raise it up at the last day.*

IN the miracle of the feeding of the five thousand our Lord presented Himself symbolically to man as the food of the soul. For, as Augustine reminds us, though the miracles wrought by our Lord are divine works, intended primarily to raise the mind from visible things to their invisible author, yet their message is not exhausted by this. They are to be interrogated also as to what they tell us about Christ, and they will be found to have a tongue of their own if we have skill to understand it. "For," he adds, "since Christ is Himself the Word of God, even a deed of the Word is a word to us." One of His miracles is accordingly not to be treated as a mere picture, which we may be satisfied to look upon and praise; but rather as a writing, which we are not content to praise though we delight in its beauty, but find no satisfaction until we have read and understood it. We may possibly consider somewhat fanciful Augustine's detailed decipherment of the signs in which this miracle is written. He discovers in it a complete parable of the salvation of man and of men. But we can scarcely refuse, as we read it in the pregnant record of

John, to say in Pauline phrase, "these things contain an allegory."

As such, indeed, John presents it. This is the meaning of his care to tell us, as he introduces his recital, that "the passover was at hand": not a mere chronological note, we may be sure ; nor yet merely an explanation of the presence of the multitude, gathered for the pilgrimage to Jerusalem ; but a premonition of what is to come, —John's account of the occasion and meaning of the miracle, which itself was the occasion of the great discourse on the bread of life. Christ, the true passover, chose the passover time, when men's minds were upon the type, to present the anti-type to them in symbol and open speech. It was therefore also that He tested His disciples with searching questions, designed to bring them to the discovery of whether they yet knew Him ; and that He taxed the people that "signs" were wasted upon them (verse 26), and that while they were demanding a sign that they might see and believe (verse 30), the sign had been given them, and though they had seen, they did not believe (verse 36). It was therefore above all, that Christ followed up the miracle with the wonderful discourse in which He explains the sign, and declares Himself openly to be "the bread of God that cometh down from heaven and giveth life to the world." This is the tremendous truth which miracle and discourse united to proclaim to the multitudes gathered on the shores of Gennesaret at that passover season ; but which, despite type and sign and teaching—each a manifest word from God,—they could neither receive nor understand. And this is the blessed truth which our text,—taken from the center of the discourse and constituting, indeed, its kernel,—presents to our apprehension and belief anew to-day. May the Spirit of truth, who searches all things, even the deep things of God, illuminate our minds and prepare our hearts, that we may understand and believe.

I. Let us begin by observing the testimony borne by our Lord and Master here to His heavenly original and descent : " I am come down from heaven," He says. And the truth here declared is the foundation of the entire discourse : the whole gist of which is to represent Jesus as the " bread out of heaven," " the true bread out of heaven," " the bread of God that cometh down out of heaven," which the Father hath given for the life of the world. I need not remind you how this representation pervades John's Gospel,—from the testimony of the Baptist (iii. 31), that He who was to supplant him " cometh from above," and is therefore " above all," to Jesus' own triumphant declaration at the close of His life, that, His work being finished, He is ready to return to the Father who sent Him, and to the glory that He had with Him before the world was (xvii. 5, 11). Our present asseveration is but a single instance of the constant self-testimony of the Son of Man to His heavenly original and descent.

The older Unitarianism was prodigal of miracle. It was not the supernatural, but the mysteries of the Holy Trinity and the God-man that were its scandal. When brought face to face with such passages as these, it was wont, therefore, to explain that Jesus, born miraculously of His virgin mother, but a mere man, was taken up to heaven by the divine power to learn the things of God ; whence He again descended to bring divine teaching to men. To the newer Unitarianism, on the other hand, it is precisely the supernatural which is the offence. Its

philosophical forms might hospitably receive such mysteries as the Trinity and the God-man, if only they may
be permitted to run freely into their moulds. But divine
interventions of any kind, and most of all the descent
of a personal God from heaven to earth, to be incased
in flesh and to herd for a season among men, it cannot
allow.   It, therefore, attacks our passages with a theory
of ideal, not real, preëxistence, and teaches that Jesus
means only that, in the thought and intention of God,
His advent into the world had long been provided for,
and that, in that sense, He was with God and came
forth from God.

How weak, how inconceivable, all such expedients
are before the majesty of Christ's self-witness : " I am
come down from heaven."   And when we turn over
the pages of this Gospel,—the leading idea of which it
has been said, inadequately indeed, but so far truly, is
the Divine glory of Christ in the incarnation,—and
observe our Lord's constant witness in the discourses
recorded in it, not merely to His descent from the
Father, but to His essential equality and oneness with
God, to His eternal preëxistence with Him, and to His
prospective return to His primal glory with the Father,
after His task on earth is accomplished,—how our spirits
bow in worship before that God only-begotten who is in
the bosom of the Father, who became flesh and taber-
nacled among us for a season full of grace and truth, and
" declared " to us by His very existence among us that
God, not only whom He came forth from, but whom
He is.

II. We should not fail to observe, however, that the
incarnation is not spoken of in our text, as an end in
itself, but rather as a means to an end.   The object of

our Lord here is not to present the bare fact of His having come down from heaven to the wonder of men, but to expound the purpose of His coming down from heaven. " I am come down from heaven," He declares, "*in order that I may do* the will of Him that sent me." You will scarcely need to be reminded that this, too, is the representation, not of our text only, but of the whole body of relevant deliverances recorded by John from the mouth of the Master, and indeed of the entire Gospel itself. Everywhere and always, it is not the coming down from heaven itself, but the purpose of the coming, that receives the emphasis. And this is why it is inadequate to say that the leading idea of John's Gospel is the glory of Christ in the incarnation. Its leading idea is, rather, the sufficient end of the incarnation, or, in other words, its leading purpose is to present what we may call a satisfactory philosophy of the incarnation.

And this is the precise amount of truth that lies behind the assertion so freely made by those who are stumbled by the heights of John's theology, that his Gospel is not a simple narrative of fact, but an ideological treatise,—which, in their view, is equivalent to saying that it does not give us fact but fancy, and is to be looked upon not as a sober history but as a metaphysical essay. But does history cease to be history when it passes beyond the mere tabulation of events, and essays to marshal them according to their relations and under the categories of cause and effect?—when it ceases to be a mere chronicle, in a word, and becomes what we have learned to call philosophical history? And is it to be made a reproach to a writer of history that he has sought not merely to collect, but also to

understand his facts ; and to record them in such a way
as to bring out their internal nature as well as their
external form ?

Bishop Alexander, in his delightful little book on
The Leading Ideas of the Gospels, places the matter
relatively to John's Gospel in a very clear light. "A
great life," he reminds us, " cannot be rendered by a
simple agglomeration of facts." " A great life,—a life
whose words and works influence mankind profoundly,—
is not sufficiently told by merely relating its facts and
dates. What an enigma, for instance, is the life of
Napoleon ! How many of his biographies are mere
masks, concealing those bronze features ! We cannot
understand any great and complicated life, good or evil,
by merely recording the isolated events along which it
moved. It is an organic whole, and must be recon-
structed as such. . . . . This, then, is the great Leading
Idea of St. John's Gospel. *Given* the facts of Christ's
life, how shall we bind them into unity, and read
them as a whole ? What theory of His Person and
Nature will give us a logical and consistent view ? . . . .
What Christ *did* and *said* becomes explicable only by
knowing what Christ *is.* . . . . Some who have not
lost all reverence for Christianity speak as if St. John's
prologue added a difficulty for faith ; as if St. Matthew
or St. Luke on the incarnation were comparatively easy
to receive. Is it so for those who think ? Place side
by side these statements. On the one side—'when as
His Mother Mary was espoused to Joseph, before they
came together she was found with child of the Holy
Ghost.' On the other side, the four oracular proposi-
tions—' in the beginning was the Word, and the Word
was with God, and the Word was God. And the

Word was made flesh.' Which is easier to receive?
. . . . In St. John the fact of the Incarnation is lifted
up and flooded with the light of a divine idea. If in
the Unity of the Divine existence there be a Trinity
of Persons; if the Second Person of that Trinity is to
assume the reality of flesh, and the likeness of sinful
flesh, we can in some measure see why He needed the
tabernacle of a body, framed and moulded by the
Eternal Spirit, to be His fitting habitation. The mystery of a Virgin Mother is the correlative of the mystery
of the Word made flesh." *

Surely this is most admirably said. To be made
quite perfect, it needs only the removal of the emphasis
from the nature of Christ to the work of Christ. "If
the Second Person of that Trinity is to assume the
reality of flesh, and the likeness of sinful flesh." . . . .
Aye, *if*. . . . . Dr. Alexander leaves this "*if*" hanging in the air. But not so John. To give an adequate
account of it is just the object and chief end of his
Gospel. We need to amend the postulation of the
problem, therefore, so far as not only to insert, but to
emphasize this element. "*Given* the facts of Christ's
life, how shall we bind them together into unity, and
read them as a whole? What theory of His Person
and Nature, and *Purpose* and *Work*, will give us a logical and consistent view?" This is the problem that
John's Gospel answers. And in answering it, it gives
us a philosophy of the incarnation, and thus renders
not only the incarnation itself, but all that Incarnated
Life, not only credible but natural, and not only natural, may we not even say? but almost inevitable—

* pp. 182–186.

impossible to be otherwise. And thus John fulfils the
end of his writing : "These are written, that ye may
believe that Jesus is the Christ, the Son of God ; and
that believing ye may have life in His name."

III. What, then, is the account of the incarnation
which this Gospel thus commends to us as its philosophy ? We note at once that in our text our Lord
states it, in the first instance, relatively not to man, but
to God. The reason of the incarnation, rendering it
credible, natural, inevitable, is traced back into the
councils of the Godhead. "I am come down from
heaven, not to do my own will, but the will of Him
that sent me."

The purpose of the incarnation is therefore primarily
to please God the Father, and to perform His will.
We cannot avoid the implication that the incarnated
one comes, therefore, in a *subordinate* capacity. He
came down from heaven not to do His own will, but the
will of Him that sent Him. He was sent. He was
given a commission, a work, to do. How this conception is repeated over and over again in the discourses
recorded by John ! Even to John the Baptist He is
the "sent of God" (John iii. 34). When Nicodemus
approached Him as a teacher come from God, He explained that He was not come primarily as a teacher,
but as one sent by God (iii. 17) to do a work. And
this is the burden of the great discourses at the pool
of Bethesda (v. 23, 36), at the feast of Tabernacles (vii.
16, 18, 28, 29), on the Light of the World (viii. 16, 18,
29, 43), and as well of the closing discourses at the last
passover (xvi. 5, xvii. 16, xviii. 33). In all alike Jesus
is the sent of God, come not of Himself (vii. 28, xviii.
43) to seek His own will, but to do the will of Him

that sent Him (v. 30) ; and only when He had "accomplished the work given Him to do" (xvii. 4) to return to the Father who sent Him (xvii. 16).

Now this subordinate relation in which Jesus thus pervasively represents Himself to have stood to the Father, so as to have been sent by Him, must be a matter either of nature or of arrangement. It must be either essential or economic. It must find its account and origin either in the necessity of nature or else in the provisions of a plan. But side by side with this perfectly pervasive proclamation of His subordination to the Father, in the whole matter of the incarnation itself, and the purpose or " will " that lies behind that incarnation and gives it its justification and its philosophical account, there runs an equally pervasive assertion by Jesus Himself and by His historian as well, of His essential equality and oneness with God. He was not only in the beginning with God : He was God. He is the only-begotten God, who is in the bosom of the Father. To have seen Him is to have seen the Father also. He draws and receives from Thomas, the worshipping cry, "My Lord and my God." He declares to the Jews, " I and the Father are One." It seems to be clear, therefore, that the subordination in which the Father is recognized as greater than He, prescribing a " will " for Him to come into the world to perform, is economic, not essential ; a matter of arrangement, not of necessity of nature.

By such a representation we are, of course, carried at once back into the darkness, or, what is equally blinding, into the blaze of mystery. It may be thought that it is enough to be asked to believe in the mysteries of the God-man and of the Trinity,—that within the unity of the Godhead there exists such a distinction of persons that of each we may assert in turn that from the beginning he has been with God, and has been God. Are we to add this additional mystery of fancying the persons of the Godhead, though numerically one in essence and sharers in all the divine attributes, "acting," as Dr. Martineau puts it, "each on the other as outside beings and conducting a divine drama among themselves,"—imposing tasks on one another, requiring conditions of one another, and earning favors from one another? No doubt it is past our comprehension. But do we gain or lose by denying its possibility, its reality? What does the Trinity mean, if it does not mean such a distinction of persons that each may say relatively to the other, "I," and "Thou," and "He"? What can the incarnation of the Second Person mean, if the persons may not stand over against one another in a measure far transcending our power to comprehend? And let us remember that John presents this conception to us, not as an added difficulty to faith, but as the philosophy, the explanation of the incarnation. It may well happen here, too, that two mysteries support and render credible each the other,—as two beams of wood, neither of which could easily stand alone, when bowed together not only support each other but provide a firm foundation upon which you may safely pile the weight of a slated roof. To adopt Bishop Alexander's mode of statement,—"If in the Unity of the Divine Existence there be a Trinity of Persons, and if the Second Person of that Trinity is to assume the reality of flesh and the likeness of sinful flesh,"—is it an additional difficulty or an aid to faith in this supernal mystery to be further told that this colossal humiliation of the Son of God was not an objectless display of arbitrary power, nor yet a tentative and unconsidered effort of divine compassion to do somewhat, as yet undetermined in kind or amount, for sinful mankind, but the execution in time of an eternal plan,—a plan born of, and redolent in its every part with the infinite compassion of God, shaped in all its details from all eternity by brooding love, and now remaining only to be executed by each person involved taking and completing his appointed part in its tremendous work? The mystery of the covenant is the correlative of the mystery of the incarnation. Without its postulation the incarnation would present increased difficulties of belief. Without the added words, " In order to do the will of Him that sent me," the declaration, " I am come down from heaven," would remain a simple marvel and prove a strain on faith.

And now let us not fail to observe that it results from what we have said, that John's Gospel is the Gospel of the Covenant. If its leading idea is not merely the glory of the incarnation, but the philosophy of the incarnation ; and if that philosophy runs back into an economic arrangement or plan between the Persons of the Trinity, by which the Second Person comes to perform a work committed to Him by the Father, not to do His own will, but the will of Him that sent Him : this is but another way of saying that the leading idea of John's Gospel is the idea of the Covenant. And is it not so? Search and look, and you will find not only that this covenant idea recurs again and again throughout the Gospel, with a frequency and an emphasis which throw it well into the foreground, but that the book, as a whole, is moulded in its form and contents upon it. The burden of its first chapters is Christ's testimony that He has come because sent by the Father ;

the burden of the last chapters is His approaching return to the Father who sent Him ; the accomplished
work lies between.   And therefore it is that when Nicodemus came to Him at the opening of His ministry
and asked for teaching, Jesus pointed him rather to His
work, and declared the doctrine of regeneration itself
"an earthly thing" compared with the heavenly mysteries He had to tell,—those mysteries of His descent from
heaven (iii. 13), sent by the Father (iii. 17) to save the
world (iii. 16).   And therefore it is that in the midst of
His ministry He opens this great discourse from which
our text is taken, by declaring that the Son of Man has
been "sealed," appointed and set apart, by the Father
for the work of giving eternal life to men ; and when
His disciples stumbled at the height of the great truth
involved,—that He had come down from heaven to give
His flesh as the food of the soul,—He sorrowfully added,
" What, then, if you should see the Son of Man ascend-
ing where He was before ? "   And therefore it is that at
the end of His life He compares His finished work with
the joy a woman has after travail, when at length the
child is born (xvi. 21) ; and declares that, having accomplished the work which the Father gave Him to do
(xvii. 21), the covenant condition is fulfilled, and the
covenanted reward is at hand, and He is about to return
to His primal glory.   John's Gospel,—we ought not to
miss it,—is the Gospel of the Covenant.

IV. How our hearts should burn within us as we
approach the last and most central question of all, and
ask what is our Lord's account of the nature and terms
of this mysterious but most blessed covenant, to fulfil
the conditions of which He came down from heaven.
We observe at once,—and with what emotions of glad-

ness we ought to observe it,—that it concerns the salvation of men. And equally at once we observe, with still swelling emotion, that it is complete and perfect in its provisions,—that it provides for an entire and finished, for a sure and unfailing salvation. And we observe that this involves—as of course it must involve—the consequence that it is definite and precise in its terms,—that it contemplates a definite and particularly designated body of men. "And this is the will of Him that sent me, that of all that He hath given me, I should lose nothing, but should raise it up at the last day." The will of the Father which Christ came down from heaven to do, concerned, then, not all men, but some men : "All that He hath given me." And His will with reference to these, which He sent the Son to perform, was not the making of some indefinite provision looking toward their rescue from sin and shame, but the definite, actual, complete, and final saving of them : that "I should lose nothing of it, but should raise it up at the last day."

Let our hearts stand still while we read these great provisions. It is the testimony of the covenanted Son Himself, as to the terms of the covenant which He came to fulfil, that it had a definite and well-defined subject,—a restricted subject if you will, a "limited" subject,—not all mankind, but a given body of men,—a given body of men who, in the text, are brought into explicit contrast with those who, though they saw, yet believed not, because they could not come to Him except the Father drew them, and He draweth none but those whom He hath given the Son and for the saving of whom the Son came down from heaven : a precisely determined body, therefore, "particularly and unchange-

ably designed, and their number so definite that it cannot be either increased or diminished." But it is as
well—and it could not be so at all, unless it were "as
well"—the testimony of the covenanted Son Himself
to the terms of the covenant which He came to fulfil,
that it had a definite and fully-determined end,—not
merely the rendering the salvation of men possible ; nor
merely the removing of the legal obstacles in the way
of the salvation of men ; nor merely the breaking down
of whatever difficulties may stand in the path of the free
outflow of God's love to men ; much less merely the
introduction into the world of a better example of life
than had hitherto been before men, or of a new divine
force making for righteousness; or the impressing of
men with a deeper sense of the love of God for them, or
of His hatred of sin ; but the actual, complete, and sure
salvation of all that the Father had given the Son :
" This is the will of Him that sent me, that all that He
hath given me, I should lose nothing of it, but should
raise it up at the last day."

In a word, we have presented to us here, in these
pregnant words, not only in outline, but in all its essential details, what has come to be known among us as
the Covenant of Redemption. Men may, no doubt,
find fault with this doctrine. They may say, as they
have said, that thus our Lord, the Saviour of the world,
is made not the Saviour of men, but only of a small,
select company of men. It does not appear with what
justification the number of those purchased by His
precious blood is represented as small, when John
represents them as an immense multitude whom no
man can number. But when the alternative is—as the
logical alternative assuredly is—limitation of the saving

work of Christ, either in its subjects or in its substance, who, on either Biblical grounds or on grounds of Christian hope and love, can hesitate one moment in his decision ? If the work of Christ is not complete, if it did not purchase for us a sure salvation, the charter of our redemption is gone. It has sometimes been thoughtlessly said that this doctrine of the Covenant of Redemption is an invention of the Reformed Theology. A distinguished professor at Andover, Dr. Park, was accustomed to tell his pupils that the Covenant was made in Holland in the middle of the seventeenth century. And a distinguished Baptist teacher, Dr. E. G. Robinson, has lately assured the religious public that the Covenant theology has been finally entombed in the grave of Charles Hodge. But not only had the doctrine of the covenants already come to its rights and been made the architectonic principle of theology, long before Cocceius published his *Sum of the Doctrine of the Covenants*, (1648)—for to him was Dr. Park alluding,—and indeed been so used, before his supposed discovery of it, in so representative a symbol as the Westminster Confession :—but from the beginning of that new discovery of the way of salvation which we call the Reformation, t had been a prominent feature in the teaching of Reformed theologians in every land. And we may well believe that it is destined to remain the central stronghold of faith to the end of time, among all who in simplicity of heart draw the matter of their teaching out of this record of our Saviour's words. For what element of the doctrine is lacking here ? " I am come down from heaven, not to do my own will, but the will of Him that sent me ": there is the assertion of an economic arrangement as the pre-

condition of the incarnation, and of the prestipulation
of the incarnated work. "And this is the will of Him
that sent me, that of all that He hath given me I should
lose nothing, but should raise it up at the last day":
there is the revelation of the contents of the pre-
incarnation arrangement, and the provision through the
incarnation for the certain salvation of a chosen body of
lost men. "All that the Father giveth me shall come
unto me"; "No man can come unto me except the
Father which sent me, draw Him": there is the twin
definition of the subjects of the salvation. Or, if we
desire further witness than this one passage, it is spread
fully on the pages of this Gospel. Let us attend only
to those calm and final words which, as His work was
accomplishing, our blessed Redeemer addressed, not to
us men, but to His Father, in a divinely assured assertion of His righteous claims upon the fruit of His work.
"Father, the hour is come: glorify thy Son, that the
Son may glorify thee: even as thou gavest Him
authority over all flesh, that to all that thou hast given
Him, He should give to them eternal life. I
glorified thee on the earth, having accomplished the
work which thou hast given me to do. And now, O
Father, glorify thou me with thine own self, with the
glory which I had with thee before the world was. I
manifested thy name unto the men whom thou didst give
me out of the world: thine they were, and thou didst
give them to me. . . . . I pray for them; I pray not
for the world, but for those whom thou hast given me."
All His work is in fulfilment of an arrangement with
the Father; and the whole of it, down to this High-
Priestly prayer itself, making intercession for His own,
concerns, primarily and in its chief import, not the

world, but those whom the Father gave Him out of the world, and secures beyond failure their complete salvation. This is the whole doctrine of the Covenant of Redemption : the Reformed theology has grasped it, and teaches it ; but it has not added one single thought to it.

And now let us bask a little, before we close, in the comforting assurances of this blessed teaching.

1. How the love of God is magnified to us by this teaching. It is not from a yesterday only that He has busied Himself with our salvation. In the depths of eternity our foreseen miseries were a cause of care to Him. In that mysterious intercourse between Father and Son, which is as eternal as the essence of Godhead itself, we—our state, our sin, our helplessness, and the dreadfulness of our condition and end,—were a subject of consideration and solicitude. What a God this is that is unveiled before us here. A God of holiness : a God so holy that even in the abyss of eternity-past He could not rest indifferent to the sin which was only after the lapse of innumerable ages, to dawn in this corner of the as yet unexistent universe. A God of justice : a God so just that already His indignation burned against the as yet uncommitted sin of such petty creatures of His will as man. But a God of love : a love so inconceivably vast as already in the profundity of the unlimited past to brood over unimaginable plans of mercy toward these few guilty wretches among the numberless multitudes of His contemplated creatures. When the Psalmist raised his eyes to the heavens above, the work of the fingers of the Almighty, and considered the moon and stars which He had ordained, he was lost in a natural wonder that so great a Creator should

concern Himself with so puny a creature : "What is man that Thou art mindful of him? And the son of man that Thou shouldst visit him?" But how much greater a marvel is before us now. It is not man as man,—a weak and puny creature—that we have to consider ; but man as sinner,—this weak and puny creature become vile and filthy, offensive and hateful to a holy and just God. It is not in contrast even with the grandeur of the worlds circling about worlds which crowd the depths of the heavens and dwarf the consequence of this speck of earth on the skirts of the universe which is our home, that we are to consider him ; but in contrast with the majesty of the increate Triune maker of all that is. It is not simply that God has taken notice of this sinful, puny creature, that we have to consider ; but that the All-Holy and All-Blessed God has felt care and solicitude for his fate and looked not at His own things in comparison with his. What indeed is sinful man that God should love him ; and before the foundations of the world should prepare to save him by so inconceivable a plan as to give His only-begotten Son as a ransom for his life! My brethren, this is not to the glory of man, but to the glory of God ; it is not the expression of our dignity and worth, but raises our wondering hearts to the contemplation of the breadth and length, and height and depth of the love of God that passeth knowledge.

2. And how our appreciation of the perfection of the work of our Saviour is enhanced by this teaching. As it was upon no sudden caprice that He came into the world, but in execution of a long-cherished and thoroughly laid plan, so it was no partial work which He performed, but the whole work of salvation. "This

is a faithful saying, and worthy of all acceptation, That
Christ Jesus came into the world to *save* sinners." And
this He has accomplished, even to the uttermost. When
He cried upon the cross, as His agony went out in the
darkness of death,—a death for us—in those words of
deepest import and of mighty power, "It is finished!"
—when in His great sacerdotal prayer, he proleptically
declared that He had "accomplished the work" which
the Father "had given Him to do," and was now ready
to lay aside His humiliation and reënter His glory : the
precise thing which He published as "finished" and
"accomplished," was salvation. All has been done by
Him. His saving work neither needs nor admits of
supplementary addition by any needy child of man,—
even to the extent of an iota. When we look to Him
we are raising grateful eyes, not to one who invites us
to save ourselves; nor merely to one who has broken
out a path, in which walking, we may attain to salvation ; nor yet merely to one who offers us a salvation
wrought out by Him, on a condition ; but to one who
has *saved* us,—who is at once the beginning and the
middle and the end of our salvation, the author and the
finisher of our faith.

What can we possibly need that we do not find provided in Him ? Do we hopelessly groan under the
curse of the broken law, hanging menacingly over us ?
Christ has "redeemed us from the curse of the law, having been made a curse for us" (Gal. iii. 13). Do we
know that only he that worketh righteousness is accept-
able to God, and despair of attaining life on so unachiev-
able a condition ? Christ Jesus "hath of God been
made unto us righteousness" (1 Cor. i. 30). Do we
loathe ourselves in the pollution of our sins, and know

that God is greater than we, and that we must be an
offence in His holy sight ? The blood of Christ cleanseth
us from all sin (1 John i. 7). But do we not need faith,
that we may be made one with Him and so secure these
benefits ? Faith, too, is the gift of God : and that we
believe on Him is granted by God in the behalf of Christ
(Phil. i. 29). Nothing has been forgotten, nothing
neglected, nothing left unprovided. In the person of
Jesus Christ, the great God, in His perfect wisdom and
unfailing power, has taken our place before the outraged
justice of God and under His perfect law, and has
wrought out a complete salvation.

3. What an indefectible certitude of salvation is
given by this great teaching. If Christ Jesus came to
save and has saved, how can salvation fail ? If the free
gift of God is eternal life in Christ Jesus our Lord
(Ro. vi. 23), how can this eternal life thus freely given
go out in time, and fail to accord with its very designa-
tion as eternal ? If Christ has undertaken not merely
to open a way of salvation to us, but to save us; if He
came into the world for the precise purpose of perform-
ing *this* will of God, " that of all that He hath given
Him, He should lose nothing, but should raise it up at
the last day,"—what possibility lies open of the failure
of this great design, framed in eternity by Triune Godhead, and executed in time by none other than the
strong Son of God? Therefore our gracious Lord
assures us : " All that the Father giveth me *shall come
unto me*, and him that cometh unto me I will in no wise
cast out." And, therefore, His servant, condescending
to the weakness of our fears, argues with us : " God
commendeth His love towards us, in that, while we
were yet sinners, Christ died for us. Much more, then,

being justified by His blood, shall we be saved from
wrath by Him." Oh, the certitude in that "much
more." "If God be for us," he argues again, "who can
be against us? He that spared not His own Son,
but delivered Him up for us all, how shall He not also
with Him, freely give us all things? .... Who shall
separate us from the love of Christ?" O weak and
trembling soul, can you not find, not courage merely,
but certitude in this? What matters your weakness?
Your salvation rests not on it, but on God's strength.
He loves you; He determined to save you; He sent
His Son to save you; He has come to do it: He has
done it. You are saved: it cannot fail, unless God's
set purpose can fail; unless Christ's power to save can
fail; unless His promises of love can fail.

4. What a clear ground of assurance of salvation is
furnished by this great teaching. Does some wayward
spirit say: "All this is true only of the elect, those whom
the Father gave to Christ. And I, alas! how may I know
that I am of the elect?" Ah, self-tormenting soul, why
expend strength in prying into God's secrets, instead of
taking Him at His word? It is true indeed that it is
only those whom He has given to Christ that Christ
has saved; and the comfort, as the salvation, is for them
alone. But it is not true that God requires of you
election for salvation, or offers you predestination as the
way of life. He offers you not predestination, but
Christ; and He requires of you not election, but faith.
Do you make election itself a ground of doubt and
despair? This, says an old Puritan, is indeed to gather
poison out of the sweetest of herbs. "God," says he,
"layeth it as a duty upon every one to repent and believe, to come to Him and he shall have rest to his

soul. . . . . If, then, thou believest, thou repentest, this
may be a sure testimony unto thee of thy everlasting
glory." So, then, "it's no wonder," he continues,
"that Paul doth often run out in large expressions concerning God's love, his predestination from all eternity"
—note how he identifies the two—"when he hath occasion to praise God for the calling and conversion of any
in time ; for this is to trace the stream till we find its
well-head." * "Madmen" is what John Calvin calls those
"who seek their salvation in the whirlpool of predestination ; not keeping the way of salvation which is
exhibited to them." "To every man," he explains,
"his faith is the sufficient proof of the eternal election
of God ; and it would be a shocking sacrilege to carry
the inquiry behind it : for an aggravated insult is offered
the Holy Spirit if we refuse to assent to His simple
testimony." †

Election does indeed lie at the root of our salvation :
but faith is the proof of election. Are we saved ? The
question is resolved in this: Do we believe in Jesus
Christ ? Christ indeed says, "This is the will of Him
who sent me, that of *all that He hath given me*, I should
lose nothing, but should raise it up at the last day."
Here is election the root of the saving work of Christ.
But have you failed to note or to remember that he
immediately adds: "For, this is the will of my Father,
that *every one that beholdeth the Son and believeth on
Him* should have eternal life, and that I should raise
him up at the last day." Here is the work of Christ

---

* A. Burgess, *Spiritual Refining*, ed. 1652, pp. 644, 593.
† *Com.* on John vi. 46.

received in faith the ground of salvation : and here is faith, laying hold of Christ, the evidence of salvation. And, therefore, it is not only said, " All that the Father giveth me shall come unto me," but it is immediately added : *"And him that cometh to me I will in no wise cast out."* These words are gracious enough in their broadest sense to send a thrill of joy through the heart. But there lies hid within them a further delicate grace which is lost in the English translation. The word for " come " is so varied in the two clauses as to lay the stress in the first instance " upon the successful issue of the coming, the arrival," and in the second "on the process of the coming and the welcome." * " All that the Father giveth me shall come unto me"—shall certainly and unfailingly reach me. "And him that cometh unto me I will in no wise cast out "—"him that is in the process of coming,"—yea, even though he is but just begun, with weak and faltering steps, even such an one as this who is but beginning to come—" I will in no wise cast out."

What a blessed assurance, when faith is made thus not the ground of salvation, not the condition of salvation, but its evidence ! It is here that the sweet herb of election begins to pour forth its refreshing cordial. Men may tell us, indeed, " Believe and you shall be saved," while still making faith the ground or the condition of salvation. And, then, with what dreadful solicitude will we pluck up our faith over and over again by the roots, to examine it with anxious fear : Is it the right faith ? Is it a strong enough faith ? Do I be-

* Westcott *in loc.*

lieve aright? Do I believe enough? Shall I abide in
my belief until the end? Dreadful uncertainty! Inex-
pressible misery of ineradicable doubt! It is only when
we have learned from such words of our Master as those
before us to-day, that we dare say to our souls not only
Believe and ye shall be saved! but those other words of
deeper meaning and fuller comfort, caught from the
Master's own blessed lips: Believe and ye *are* saved!
"Verily, verily, I say unto you," says our Saviour in
words which sum up previous teachings (John iii. 18,
36): "He that heareth my words and believeth Him
that sent me, *hath* eternal life, and cometh not into
judgment but *hath* passed out of death into life."
Blessed John, who so caught his Master's words and recorded them for us.   When faith is thus made not the
ground or the condition, but the evidence of salvation,
our eternal bliss is no longer suspended in any sense on
aught that we are or do, but hangs solely on the work
of Christ, doing His Father's will.   Faith, even faith, as
the ground or condition of salvation, may be also the
ground of despair: but faith as the proof of salvation is
the charter of assured though humble hope.   It takes
hold of the "strong Son of God, immortal love," and
of the indefectible purpose of Almighty grace which
cannot fail or know any shadow of turning.   This we
owe to that doctrine of the eternal covenant which our
blessed Saviour reveals to us in the words on which we
have meditated to-day.   Because of its blessed provisions we can cry joy to our souls, though they trem-
ble with natural fear and can scarce believe that Christ
will save such faithless souls as they.   Though they have
faith but as a grain of mustard-seed, they *are* saved

already. For, this is the will of Him who sent our Redeemer, that of all that He gave Him, He should lose nothing, but should raise it up at the last day : for this is the will of the Father that every one that beholdeth the Son and believeth on Him should have eternal life and He should raise him up at the last day.

II.

THE EXAMPLE OF THE INCARNATION.

II.

THE EXAMPLE OF THE INCARNATION.

PHILIPPIANS ii. 5–8 : *Let this mind be in you, which was also in Christ Jesus ; who, being in the form of God, thought it not robbery to be equal with God : but made himself of no reputation, and took upon him the form of a servant, and was made in the likeness of men : and being found in fashion as a man, he humbled himself, and became obedient unto death, even the death of the cross.*

"CHRIST our Example ": after "Christ our Redeemer," no words can more deeply stir the Christian heart than these. Every Christian joyfully recognizes the example of Christ, as, in the admirable words of a great Scotch commentator, a body " of living legislation," as " law, embodied and pictured in a perfect humanity." In Him, in a word, we find the moral ideal historically realized, and we bow before it as sublime and yearn after it with all the assembled desires of our renewed souls.

How lovingly we follow in thought every footstep of the Son of Man, on the rim of hills that shut in the emerald cup of Nazareth, on the blue marge of Gennesaret, over the mountains of Judea, and long to walk in spirit by His side. He came to save every age, says Irenæus, and therefore He came as an infant, a child, a boy, a youth, and a man. And there is no age that cannot find its example in Him. We see Him, the properest child that ever was given to a mother's arms, through all the years of childhood at Nazareth "subjecting Himself to His parents." We see Him a youth, labor-

ing day by day contentedly at His father's bench, in this
lower sphere, too, with no other thought than to be
"about His father's business." We see Him in His
holy manhood, going, "as His custom was," Sabbath
by Sabbath, to the synagogue,—God as He was, not too
good to worship with His weaker brethren.   And then
the horizon broadens.   We see Him at the banks of
Jordan, because it became Him to fulfil every righteousness, meekly receiving the baptism of repentance for us.
We see Him in the wilderness, calmly rejecting the
subtlest trials of the evil one : refusing to supply His
needs by a misuse of His divine power, repelling the
confusion of tempting God with trusting God, declining
to seek His Father's ends by any other than His Father's
means.   We see Him among the thousands of Galilee,
anointed of God with the Holy Ghost and power, going
about doing good : with no pride of birth, though He
was a king ; with no pride of intellect, though omni-
science dwelt within Him; with no pride of power, though
all power in Heaven and earth was in His hands ; or of
station, though the fulness of the Godhead dwelt in
Him bodily ; or of superior goodness or holiness : but
in lowliness of mind esteeming every one better than
Himself, healing the sick, casting out devils, feeding the
hungry, and everywhere breaking to men the bread of
life.   We see Him everywhere offering to men His life
for the salvation of their souls : and when, at last, the
forces of evil gathered thick around Him, walking, alike
without display and dismay, the path of suffering
appointed for Him, and giving His life at Calvary that
through His death the world might live.

    "Which of you convinceth me of sin ?" is too low a
question.   Who can find in all His life a single lack, a

single failure to set us a perfect example? In what
difficulty of life, in what trial, in what danger or uncertainty, when we turn our eyes to Him, do we fail to find
just the example that we need? And if perchance
we are, by the grace of God, enabled to walk with Him
but a step in the way, how our hearts burn within us
with longing to be always with Him,—to be strength-
ened by the almighty power of God in the inner man,
to make every footprint which He has left in the world
a stepping-stone to climb upward over His divine path.
Do we not rightly say that next to our longing to be in
Christ is our corresponding longing to be like Christ;
that only second in our hearts to His great act of obedience unto death by which He became our Saviour,
stands His holy life in our world of sin, by which He
becomes our example?

Of course our text is not singular in calling upon us
to make Christ our example. " Be ye imitators of me,
even as I also am of Christ Jesus," is rather the whole
burden of the ethical side of Paul's teaching. And in
this, too, he was but the imitator of his Lord, who
pleads with us to " learn of Him because He is meek
and lowly in heart." The peculiarity of our present
passage is that it takes us back of Christ's earthly life
and bids us imitate Him in the great act of His incarnation itself. Not, of course, as if the implication were
that we were equal with Christ and needed to stoop to
such service as He performed. " Why art thou proud,
O man?" Augustine asks pointedly. " God for thee
became low. Thou wouldst perhaps be ashamed to imitate a lowly man; then at least imitate the lowly God.
The Son of God came in the character of man and was
made low. . . . . He, since He was God, became man :

do thou, O man, recognize that thou art man. Thy entire humility is to know thyself." The very force of the
appeal lies, in a word, in the infinite exaltation of Christ
above us: and the mention of the incarnation is the
Apostle's reminder to us of the ineffable majesty which
was by nature His to whom he would raise our admir-
ing eyes. Paul pries at our hearts here with the great
lever of the deity of our exemplar. He calls upon us
to do nothing less than to be imitators of God. "What
encouragement is greater than this?" cries Chrysostom,
with his instinctive perception of the motive-springs of
the human heart. "Nothing arouses a great soul to the
performance of good works, so much as learning that
in this it is likened to God." And here, too, Paul is but
the follower of his Lord: "Be ye merciful, as your
Father which is in heaven is merciful," are words which
fell from His divine lips, altogether similar in their implication to Paul's words in the text: "Let it be this mind
that is in you, which also was in Christ Jesus." It is
the Spirit which animated our Lord in the act of His
incarnation which His apostle would see us imitate. He
would have us in all our acts to be like Christ, as He
showed Himself to be in the innermost core of His being, when He became poor, He that was rich, that we
by His poverty might be made rich.

We perceive, then, that the exhortation of the Apostle
gathers force for itself from the deity of Christ, and
from the nature of the transaction by which He, being
God, was brought into this sphere of dependent, earthly
life in which we live by nature. It is altogether natural, then, that he sharpens his appeal by reminding his
readers somewhat fully who Christ was and what He did
for our salvation, in order that, having the facts more

vividly before their minds, they may more acutely feel
the spirit by which He was animated. Thus, in a perfectly natural way, Paul is led, not to inform his readers
but to remind them, in a few quick and lively phrases
which do not interrupt the main lines of discourse but
rather etch them in with a deeper color, of what we may
call the whole doctrine of the Person of Christ. With
such a masterly hand, or let us rather say with such an
eager spirit and such a loving clearness and firmness of
touch, has he done this, that these few purely incidental
words constitute one of the most complete statements of
an essential doctrine to be found within the whole com-
pass of the Scriptures. Though compressed within the
limits of three short verses, it ranks in fulness of exposi-
tion with the already marvellously concise outline of the
same doctrine given in the opening verses of the Gospel
of John. Whenever the subtleties of heresy confuse our
minds as we face the problems which have been raised
about the Person of our Lord, it is preëminently to
these verses that we flee to have our apprehension
purified, and our thinking corrected. The sharp phrases
cut their way through every error: or, as we may better
say, they are like a flight of swift arrows, each winged
to the joints of the harness.

The golden-mouthed preacher of the ancient church,
impressed with this fulness of teaching and inspired
himself to one of his loftiest flights by the verve of the
Apostle's crisp language, pictures the passage itself as
an arena, and the Truth, as it runs burning through the
clauses, as the victorious chariot dashing against and
overthrowing its contestants one after the other, until
at last, amid the clamor of applause which rises from
every side to heaven, it springs alone towards the goal,

with coursers winged with joy sweeping like a single flash over the ground.   One by one he points out the heresies concerning the Person of Christ which had sprung up in the ancient church, as clause by clause the text smites and destroys them ; and is not content until he shows how the knees of all half-truths and whole falsehoods alike concerning this great matter are made by these searching words to bow before our Saviour's perfect deity, His complete humanity, and the unity of His person.   The magic of the passage has lost none of its virtue with the millennium and a half which has fled by since John electrified Constantinople with his golden words : this sword of the Spirit is as keen to-day as it was then, and happy is the man who knows its temper and has the arm to wield it.   But we must not lose ourselves in a purely theological interest with such a passage before us.   Rather let us keep our eyes, for this hour, on Paul's main purpose, and seek to feel the force of the example of Christ as he here ad-vances it, for the government of our lives.   But to do this, as he points it with so full a reference to the Person of Christ, following him we must begin by striving to realize who and what our Lord was, who set us this ex-ample.

I. Let us observe, then, first, that the actor to whose example Paul would direct our eyes, is declared by him to have been no other than God Himself.   "Who was before in the form of God," are his words : and they are words than which no others could be chosen which would more explicitly or with more directness assert the deity of the person who is here designated by the name of Christ Jesus.   After the wear and tear of two thousand years on the phrases, it would not be surprising if we should fail to feel this as strongly as we ought. Let us remember that the phraseology which Paul here employs was the popular usage of his day, though first given general vogue by the Aristotelian philosophy : and that it was accordingly the most natural language for strongly asserting the deity of Christ which could suggest itself to him. As you know, this mode of speech resolved everything into its matter and its form, —into the bare material out of which it is made, and that body of characterizing qualities which constitute it what it is. " Form," in a word, is equivalent to our phrase, " specific character." If we may illustrate great things by small, we may say, in this manner of speech, that the " matter ' of a sword, for instance, is steel, while its " form " is that whole body of characterizing qualities which distinguish a sword from all other pieces of steel, and which, therefore, make this particular piece of steel distinctively a sword. In this case, these are, of course, largely matters of shape and contour. But now the steel itself, which constitutes the matter of the sword, has also its " matter " and its " form ": its " matter " being metal, and its " form " being the whole body of qualities that distinguish steel from other metals, and make this metal steel. Going back still a step, metal itself has its " matter " and " form "; its " matter " being material substance and its " form " that body of qualities which distinguish metallic from other kinds of substance. And last of all, matter itself has its " matter," namely, substance, and its " form," namely, the qualities which distinguish material from spiritual substance, and make this substance what we call matter. The same mode of speech is, of course, equally applicable to the spiritual sphere. The " matter " of the human spirit is

bare spiritual substance, while its "form" is that body
of qualities which constitute this spirit a human spirit,
and in the absence of which, or by the change of which,
this spirit would cease to be human and become some
other kind of spirit.   The "matter" of an angel, again,
is bare spiritual substance, while the "form" is the body
of qualities which make this spirit specifically an angel.
So, too, with God : the "matter" of God is bare spiritual substance, and the "form" is that body of qualities
which distinguish Him from all other spiritual beings,
which constitute Him God, and without which He
would not be God.   What Paul asserts then, when he
says that Christ Jesus existed in the "form of God," is
that He had all those characterizing qualities which make
God God, the presence of which constitutes God, and
in the absence of which God does not exist.   He who
is "in the form of God," is God.

Nor is it without significance that, out of the possible
modes of expression open to him, Paul was led to choose
just this mode of asserting the deity of our Lord.   His
mind in this passage was not on the bare divine essence ;
it was upon the divine qualities and prerogatives of
Christ.   It is not the abstract conception that Christ is
God that moves us to our deepest admiration for His
sublime act of self-sacrifice: but rather our concrete
realization that He was all that God is, and had all that
God has,—that God's omnipotence was His, His infinite
exaltation, His unapproachable blessedness.   Therefore
Paul is instinctively led to choose an expression which
tells us not the bare fact that Christ was God, but that
He was "in the form of God,"—that He had in full
possession all those characterizing qualities which, taken
together, make God that all-holy, perfect, all-blessed be-

ing which we call God. Thus the Apostle prepares his readers for the great example by quickening their apprehension not only of who, but of what Christ was.

II. Let us note, then, secondly, that the Apostle outlines for us very fully the action which this divine being performed. " He took the form of a servant by coming into the likeness of men ; and being found in fashion as a man, He humbled Himself by becoming subject even unto death, and that the death of the cross." There is no metamorphosis of substance asserted here : the " form of God " is not said to have been transmuted into the "form of a servant"; but He who was " in the form of God " is declared to have taken also to Himself " the form of a servant." Nor is there, on the other hand, any deceptive show of an unreal humiliation brought before us here : He took, not the appearance, mere state and circumstances, or mere work and performance, but veritably " the form of a servant,"—all those essential qualities and attributes which belong to, and constitute a being " a servant." The assumption involved the taking of an actually servile nature, as well as of a subordinate station and a servant's work. And therefore it is at once further explained in both its mode and its effects. He took the form of a servant " by coming into the likeness of men ": He did not become merely a man, but by taking the form of a servant He came into a state in which He appeared as man. His humanity was real and complete : but it was not all,—He remained God in assuming humanity, and therefore only appeared as man, not became only man. And by taking the form of a servant and thus being found in fashion as a man, He became subject to obedience,—an obedience pressed so far in its humiliation that it extended even unto

death, and that the shameful death of the cross. Words
cannot adequately paint the depth of this humiliation.
But this it was,—the taking of the form of a servant
with its resultant necessity of obedience to such a bitter
end,—this it was that He who was by nature in the
form of God,—in the full possession and use of all the
Divine attributes and qualities, powers, and prerogatives,
—was willing to do for us.

III. Let us observe, then, thirdly, that the Apostle
clearly announces to us the spirit in which our Lord
performed this great act. "Although He was in the
form of God, He yet did not consider His being on an
equality with God a precious prize to be eagerly retained,
but made no account of Himself, taking the form of a
servant." It was then in a spirit of pure unselfishness
and self-sacrifice, that looked not on its own things but
on the things of others, that under the force of love
esteemed others more than Himself,—it was in this
mind : or, in the Apostle's own words, it was as not con-
sidering His essential equality with God as a precious
possession, but making no account of Himself,—it was
in this mind, that Christ Jesus who was before in the form
of God took the form of a servant. This was the state
of mind that led Him to so marvellous an act,—no com-
pulsion from His Father, no desires for Himself, no
hope of gain or fear of loss, but simple, unselfish, self-
sacrificing love.

Now it is not to be overlooked that some of the
clauses the meaning of which we have sought to fathom,
are differently explained among expositors. Nevertheless, although I have sought to adduce them so as to
bring out the Apostle's exact meaning, and although I
believe that his appeal acquires an additional point and

a stronger leverage when they are thus understood, it remains true that the main drift of the passage is unaffected by any of the special interpretations which reasonable expositors have put upon the several clauses. These divergent expositions do seriously affect our doctrine of the Person of Christ. In particular, all the forms of the popular modern doctrine of *Kenosis* or *Exinanition*, which teaches that the divine Logos in becoming man "emptied Himself," and thus, that the very God in a more or less literal sense contracted Himself to the limits of humanity, find their chief, almost their sole Biblical basis in what appears to me a gratuitously erroneous interpretation of one of these clauses,—that one which the Authorized Version renders, "He made Himself of no reputation," and which I have ventured to render, "He made no account of Himself," that is, in comparison with the needs of others; but which the theologians in question followed, unfortunately as I think, by the Revised Version, render with an excessive literality, "He emptied Himself," thereby resurrecting the literal physical sense of the word in an unnatural context. We have many reasons to give why this is an illegitimate rendering; chief among which are, that the word is commonly employed in its figurative sense and that the intrusion of the literal sense here is forbidden by the context. But it is unnecessary to pause to argue the point. Whatever the conclusion might be, the main drift of the passage remains the same. No interpretation of this phrase can destroy the outstanding fact that the passage at large places before our wondering eyes the two *termini* of "the form of God" and "the form of a servant," involving obedience even unto a shameful death; and "measures the extent of our

Lord's self-denying grace by the distance between equality with God and a public execution on a gibbet." * In any case the emphasis of the passage is thrown upon the spirit of self-sacrificing unselfishness as the impelling cause of Christ's humiliation, which the Apostle adduces here in order that the sight of it may impel us also to take no account of ourselves, but to estimate lightly all that we are or have in comparison with the claims of others on our love and devotion. The one subject of the whole passage is Christ's marvellous self-sacrifice. Its one exhortation is, " Let it be this mind that is also in you." As we read through the passage we may, by contact with the full mind and heart of the Apostle, learn much more than this. But let us not fail to grasp this, his chief message to us here,—that Christ Jesus, though He was God, yet cared less for His equality with God, cared less for Himself and His own things, than He did for us, and therefore gave Himself for us.

Firmly grasping this, then, as the essential content and special message of the passage, there are some inferences that flow from it which we cannot afford not to remind ourselves of.

1. And first of these is a very great and marvellous one,—that we have a God who is capable of self-sacrifice for us. It was although He was in the form of God, that Christ Jesus did not consider His being on an equality with God so precious a possession that He could not lay it aside, but rather made no account of Himself. It was our God who so loved us that He gave Himself for us. Now, herein is a wonderful thing. Men tell us that God is, by the very necessity of His

---

* The phraseology here is borrowed from Eadie's *Com.* in loc.

nature, incapable of passion, incapable of being moved by inducements from without; that He dwells in holy calm and unchangeable blessedness, untouched by human sufferings or human sorrows forever,—haunting

> " The lucid interspace of world and world,
> Where never creeps a cloud, nor moves a wind,
> Nor ever falls the least white star of snow,
> Nor ever lowest roll of thunder moans,
> Nor sound of human sorrow mounts to mar
> His sacred, everlasting calm."

Let us bless our God that it is not true. God can feel; God does love. We have Scriptural warrant for believing, as it has been well phrased, that moral heroism has a place within the sphere of the Divine nature: we have Scriptural warrant for believing that, like the old hero of Zurich, God has reached out loving arms and gathered into His own bosom that forest of darts which otherwise had pierced ours.

But is not this gross anthropomorphism? We are careless of names : it is the truth of God. And we decline to yield up the God of the Bible and the God of our hearts to any philosophical abstraction. We have and we must have an ethical God; a God whom we can love, and in whom we can trust. We may feel awe in the presence of the Absolute, as we feel awe in the presence of the storm or of the earthquake: we may feel our dependence in its presence, as we feel our helplessness before the tornado or the flood. But we cannot love it ; we cannot trust it ; and our hearts, which are just as trustworthy a guide as our dialectics, cry out for a God whom we may love and trust. We decline once for all to subject our whole conception of God to the category of the Absolute, which, as has been truly

said, "like Pharaoh's lean kine, devours all other attributes."* Neither is this an unphilosophical procedure.
As has recently been set forth renewedly by Andrew
Seth,† "we should be unfaithful to the fundamental
principle of the theory of knowledge " " if we did not
interpret by means of the highest category within our
reach." " We should be false to ourselves, if we denied
in God what we recognize as the source of dignity and
worth in ourselves." In order to escape an anthropo-
morphic God, we must not throw ourselves at the feet
of a zoömorphic or an amorphic one.

Nevertheless, let us rejoice that our God has not left
us by searching to find Him out. Let us rejoice that
He has plainly revealed Himself to us in His Word as
a God who loves us, and who, because He loves us, has
sacrificed Himself for us. Let us remember that the
fundamental conception in the Christian idea of God is
that God is love ; and the fundamental dogma of the
Christian religion is that God so loved us that He gave
Himself for us. Accordingly, the primary presupposi-
tion of our present passage is that our God was capable
of, and did actually perform, this amazing act of unselfish self-sacrifice for the good of man.

2. The second inference that we should draw from
our passage consists simply in following the Apostle in
his application of this divine example to our human
life : a life of self-sacrificing unselfishness is the most
divinely beautiful life that man can lead. He whom as
our Master we have engaged to obey, whom as our
Example we are pledged to imitate, is presented to us
here as the great model of self-sacrificing unselfishness.

* By Prof. A. B. Bruce, in his *Humiliation of Christ.*
† *Hegelianism and Personality*, p. 222.

" Let this mind be in you, which was also in Christ Jesus," is the Apostle's pleading. We need to note carefully, however, that it is not self-depreciation, but self-abnegation, that is thus commended to us. If we would follow Christ, we must, every one of us, not in pride but in humility, yet not in lowness but in lowliness, not degrade ourselves but forget ourselves, and seek every man not his own things but those of others.

Who does not see that in this organism which we call human society, such a mode of life is the condition of all real help and health ? There is, no doubt, another ideal of life far more grateful to our fallen human nature, an ideal based on arrogance, assumption, self-assertion, working through strife, and issuing in conquest,—conquest of a place for ourselves, a position, the admiration of man, power over men. We see its working on every side of us : in the competition of business life,—in the struggle for wealth on the one side, forcing a struggle for bare bread on the other ; in social life,—in the fierce battle of men and women for leading parts in the farce of social display ; even in the church itself, and among the churches, where, too, unhappily, arrogant pretension and unchristian self-assertion do not fail to find their temporal reward. But it is clear that this is not Christ's ideal, nor is it to this that He has set us His perfect example. " He made no account of Himself": though He was in the form of God, He yet looked not upon His equality with God as a possession to be prized when He could by forgetting self rescue those whom He was not ashamed, amid all His glory, to call His brethren.

Are there any whom you and I are ashamed to call our brethren ? O that the divine ideal of life as service could take possession of our souls! O that we could remember at all times and in all relations that the Son of Man came into the world to minister, and by His ministry has glorified all ministering for ever. O that we could once for all grasp the meaning of the great fact that self-forgetfulness and self-sacrifice express the divine ideals of life.

3. And thus we are led to a third inference, which comes to us from the text : that it is difficult to set a limit to the self-sacrifice which the example of Christ calls upon us to be ready to undergo for the good of our brethren. It is comparatively easy to recognize that the ideal of the Christian life is self-sacrificing unselfishness, and to allow that it is required of those who seek to enter into it, to subordinate self and to seek first the kingdom of God. But is it so easy to acknowledge, even to ourselves, that this is to be read not generally merely but in detail, and is to be applied not only to some eminent saints but to all who would be Christ's servants ?—that it is required of us, and that what is required of us is not some self-denial but all self-sacrifice ? Yet is it not to this that the example of Christ would lead us ?—not, of course, to self-degradation, not to self-effacement exactly, but to complete self-abnegation, entire and ungrudging self-sacrifice ? Is it to be unto death itself ? Christ died. Are we to endure wrongs ? What wrongs did He not meekly bear ? Are we to surrender our clear and recognized rights ? Did Christ stand upon His unquestioned right of retaining His equality with God ? Are we to endure unnatural evils, permit ourselves to be driven into inappropriate situations, unresistingly sustain injurious and unjust imputations and attacks ? What more unnatural

than that the God of the universe should become a
servant in the world, ministering not to His Father only,
but also to His creatures,—our Lord and Master wash-
ing our very feet? What more abhorrent than that
God should die? There is no length to which Christ's
self-sacrifice did not lead Him. These words are dull
and inexpressive; we cannot enter into thoughts so high.
He who was in the form of God took such thought
for us, that He made no account of Himself. Into the
immeasurable calm of the divine blessedness He permitted this thought to enter, "I will die for men!"
And so mighty was His love, so colossal the divine
purpose to save, that He thought nothing of His
divine majesty, nothing of His unsullied blessedness,
nothing of His equality with God, but, absorbed in us,—
our needs, our misery, our helplessness—He made no
account of Himself. If this is to be our example, what
limit can we set to our self-sacrifice? Let us remember
that we are no longer our own but Christ's, bought
with the price of His precious blood, and are hence-
forth to live, not for ourselves but for Him,—for Him in
His creatures, serving Him in serving them. Let all
thought of our dignity, our possessions, our rights,
perish out of sight, when Christ's service calls to us.
Let the mind be in us that was also in Him, when He
took no account of Himself, but, God as He was, took
the form of a servant and humbled Himself,—He who
was Lord,—to lowly obedience even unto death, and
that the death of the cross. In such a mind as this,
where is the end of unselfishness?

4. Let us not, however, do the Apostle the injustice
of fancying that this is a morbid life to which he summons
us. The self-sacrifice to which he exhorts us, unlimited

as it is, going all lengths and starting back blanched at nothing, is nevertheless not an unnatural life. After all, it issues not in the destruction of self, but only in the destruction of selfishness; it leads us not to a Buddha-like unselfing, but to a Christ-like self-development. It would not make us into

> "deedless dreamers lazying out a life
> Of self-suppression, not of selfless love"

but would light the flames of a love within us by which we would literally "ache for souls." The example of Christ and the exhortation of Paul found themselves upon a sense of the unspeakable value of souls. Our Lord took no account of Himself, only because the value of the souls of men pressed upon His heart. And following Him, we are not to consider our own things, but those of others, just because everything earthly that concerns us is as nothing compared with their eternal welfare.

Our self-abnegation is thus not for our own sake, but for the sake of others. And thus it is not to mere self-denial that Christ calls us, but specifically to self-sacrifice: not to unselfing ourselves, but to unselfishing ourselves. Self-denial for its own sake is in its very nature ascetic, monkish. It concentrates our whole attention on self—self-knowledge, self-control—and can, therefore, eventuate in nothing other than the very apotheosis of selfishness. At best it succeeds only in subjecting the outer self to the inner self, or the lower self to the higher self; and only the more surely falls into the slough of self-seeking, that it partially conceals the selfishness of its goal by refining its ideal of self and excluding its grosser and more outward elements. Self-

denial, then, drives to the cloister; narrows and con-
tracts the soul; murders within us all innocent desires,
dries up all the springs of sympathy, and nurses and
coddles our self-importance until we grow so great in
our own esteem as to be careless of the trials and sufferings, the joys and aspirations, the strivings and
failures and successes of our fellow-men. Self-denial,
thus understood, will make us cold, hard, unsympathetic,
—proud, arrogant, self-esteeming,—fanatical, overbear-
ing, cruel. It may make monks and Stoics,—it cannot
make Christians.

It is not to this that Christ's example calls us. He
did not cultivate self, even His divine self: He took no
account of self. He was not led by His divine impulse
out of the world, driven back into the recesses of His
own soul to brood morbidly over His own needs, until
to gain His own seemed worth all sacrifice to Him.
He was led by His love for others into the world, to
forget Himself in the needs of others, to sacrifice self
once for all upon the altar of sympathy. Self-sacrifice
brought Christ into the world. And self-sacrifice will
lead us, His followers, not away from but into the
midst of men. Wherever men suffer, there will we be
to comfort. Wherever men strive, there we will be to
help. Wherever men fail, there will we be to uplift.
Wherever men succeed, there will we be to rejoice.
Self-sacrifice means not indifference to our times and
our fellows: it means absorption in them. It means
forgetfulness of self in others. It means entering into
every man's hopes and fears, longings and despairs: it
means manysidedness of spirit, multiform activity, mul-
tiplicity of sympathies. It means richness of development. It means not that we should live one life, but a

thousand lives,—binding ourselves to a thousand souls
by the filaments of so loving a sympathy that their
lives become ours.   It means that all the experiences
of men shall smite our souls and shall beat and batter
these stubborn hearts of ours into fitness for their
heavenly home.   It is, after all, then, the path to the
highest possible development, by which alone we can be
made truly men.

Not that we shall undertake it with this end in view.
This were to dry up its springs at their source.   We
cannot be self-consciously self-forgetful, selfishly unselfish.   Only, when we humbly walk this path, seeking
truly in it not our own things but those of others, we
shall find the promise true, that he who loses his life
shall find it.   Only, when, like Christ, and in loving
obedience to His call and example, we take no account
of ourselves, but freely give ourselves to others, we shall
find, each in his measure, the saying true of himself also :
" Wherefore also God hath highly exalted him."   The
path of self-sacrifice is the path to glory.